VOIR DIRE

NICO VASSILAKIS

VOIR DIRE

NICO VASSILAKIS

This is a DUSIE book.

Copyright 2020, Nico Vassilakis

Cover image, *Letter Composition 2014,* by the author.
Layout and book design: DUSIE | dusie.org

Poems have appeared in the following publications:
*A Dozen Nothing, Brave New Word, Erotoplasty, Lune,
Leere Mitte, Niedern Gasse, Pageboy and Utsanga.*

The author and press thanks the editors of these
 publications.

Dusie books are printed by Ingram. Books may be
purchased online via the distributors or ordered
directly from the press. whenever possible, please
order through independent bookstores and libraries.

Library of Congress cataloging-in-publication data
Vassilakis, Nico
Voir Dire/ Nico Vassilakis — 1st american ed.

ISBN: 978-1-944253-08-0
LCCN: 2020941983

10 9 8 7 6 5 4 3 2 1

811.6 American poetry—21st century.
2. American poet—21st century. 3. Vispo—21st
century.

CONTENT

THEN THERE WAS YOU

I like to think of myself as a verb.
A vowel even

I saw another bird in the side-view mirror today
Obsessed with its reflection

There's this measure of
Something we carry
Around with us

What is
Is jumbled
And mumbling

Of listening
To noise

Spoke frequently
With gained momentum
And choice patterns

At a distance
It was rain hitting
The awning

Sits alone now
Without access to
Enough window

What is it to leave here
With no pencil to
Mark the way

*

Local interference

Vision is pliable
A glockenspiel in fog

They don't intend to berate you,
but they're going to berate you
and they'll feel terrible about themselves

The surface is dangerous.
Always more so behind the drapes

Words destabilize
Letters get radicalized
Everything becomes visual

Even that now is passé

Plate #24
(X)

A single unit, one glee, a circle,
is subject to 'dynamic' analysis
and appears to us in differing points
of transformation

My money's not long enough
You need long money to hear that music
How much does the Hudson River weigh?
I think there's something faster than light -
the speed of light, I mean

The silver tsunami is coming

They won't look at me
Even with their eyes closed

Life is not ours
It belongs to the master
padlock above

What was once an impossibly
tiny group has grown a thousand-fold

Raucous and varied, the tuba has
too much metal - all that metal to blow through

Stop falling against yourself
Dying is unfinished business

I handwrite in small notebooks
as a shield to protect me from
the surrounding noise and chaos

An adventure that includes
a fill-in-the-blank section

All around me shiny tiny
little lights full of *doh re me doh*

Hey Glee, you will be expected
to catch the letters as they are
ejected from the word

They made a concoction
that surpassed all expectations
of what is currently knowable

An abyss on full alert
A rum-soaked phrase generator
A tunnel cloaked as vortex

I will conquer this encounter

Drizzled and rattled

Trounced and pulverized

So what? I hate symmetry
And so what? I'm not a fan of mail art
But really, I can't stand your ego

Imagine laughing caused by
everything being new again
like the hilarity of seeing it
for the first time

*

Hobart, the staring baby, whispers 'infinity' over
and over again

An unreadable text
creates a landscape you're invited to engage

Things have changed since this this

But my horses are jumping
running out of paper now

Our optical landmarks continue to form and
disintegrate. It's easy to understand how someone
might be simultaneously lost and found

Each poet different from the next - an idea-
accumulating posture

It's maddening

When was that machine built?
That machine over there for making babies

I don't know when it was built
but I've been to three funerals so far

Madge, you're soaking in it

The snippets of a lived experience watched from
across the street

A privacy to die for
My private weather event

A walk, thought chaos. A pile of uncharted
articulations your brain is readying to meet.
A walker through chaos

Under closer scrutiny, templates never align.
You can leave now, we have figured it out

*

15

Crazy people are coming
Crazy people are here

Are you the king of lymph nodes?

It's good to be busy and creative

There's an eye in my lollipop

Please don't let me die now. Maybe later, but not
now. Can you promise me that?

How are you this morning?

Well, I haven't seen her for three days now

Confusion is her baseline

William HOWARD Taft married
one of the Romanovs to start a new colony

Oi Oi Oi

Stuttering in your dreams

I just might be caught in such lack of initiative
that conversations make for the most
uncomfortable part of the day

The administering of it

A foul stench stretching out into the day

We're an amalgam of unrelated gestures,
separate and sequential, it's who we are, how the
day's noise gets made

Hey writing, I don't know you anymore

*

Several fronts
Several fonts
Gnawed through
The human condition's
Extreme
When aroused

It's not a crime to be
Strange

His middle name is Falcon

Hanging half out the window over the parking lot
Followed by the clubhouse stairs

I'm out of the office and no longer active
in cultural event business

Language flag
Language flags

Our interactions with machines have created a
divide. You speak like you think I'm stupid

J Crew Factory

Where did you get those flats? *J Crew Factory*

They look so comfortable, plus they have a heel.
Yeah, go online and use the ebate discount code

To where?   *J Crew Factory*

*Electro-formatt*ed cognition
In my isolation
It's imperative you vote
Despite social media
Thanks for staring

This and Thisism

Thanks for sharing

*

So many double agents have gone

I just respond better to people

The soundtrack of tonal inflection and guitars

Talking, talking around me

Man is meant to have arguments

If you think too long, you think wrong

Something about audio metaphors

That structure there goes like this and this and
this - I thought I invented that

They steal big computers
The devil is in the moon and has large wings
The devils go anywhere

My fingers don't say anything
My fingers don't talk

Not very Jerry
Not very obbligato

There's a science to openness

One of these lucky days I'll be dead
One of these lucky days will change everything

"He attracted some attention when he found the
fourth dimension"

Agendas in forms of seeing.
To weaponize seeing and cajoling with radical
statistics. Putting yourself in a position to see
things. Different things. To see differences, slight
variations of the original

It starts with one person taking a leap and
another person catching that person. Over and
over, taking turns till the impulse to leap softens
and quiet engulfs all

I don't know what to write, but know something
needs writing

The distance is getting louder. I think I'll choose
just the right words to alleviate this load I'm carrying
That won't happen until I start You might think this is
starting, but it's not, it's a ruse

I know I'll be getting up to have a cigarette, make
some tea, survey the grounds. I will divert in expert
fashion

I wonder about my friends, I actively don't call them.
Distraction is my sidekick

How we engage with our digital selves and how we
distract ourselves to avoid the germ of awareness

The unpredictable is an instigator. This might keep
me writing, but I'll need accelerants to sustain that

This tiny novel is going nowhere
I'm bored already

*

In a nearer future

There will be no choice

The new economy will be less, much less

*

They have become ghost cutouts in a pop-up
house I built in quiet. When a part of your engine
falls away, it is not easily replaced. This part did the
heavy lifting, was the shoulder of the operation.
Nothingness seems to be evolving further.
I offer here a Surplus of Letters

*

Where the curtains kick one another
Amazing how music speaks to you
I love those clouds
Are those buildings clouds?
The music is too good to enjoy
It's soft, soft as cotton
So fast the eye can't pick it up
We're just going to walk a little ways up here till
we get to the museum of alcoholics
He's got a tumor on his tongue

*

When did you arrive? When did the pain start?
What type of work did you do in your life? I was
asleep. Do you know how this machine works?
Which one?

The wasted years of ignorance or trying to get
beyond consciousness

He was square and nothing else and
you knew he was there

I said, hey, there's no green in that shirt. The eel
has a very strong mouth and muscular tail. The
river is the same - I discuss with you entirely

Nothingness seems to be evolving again.
Fragments are in constant collision. Uncertainty
is life with no fear

This environment is not poetry. It is rambling
lodged in your eye

When did you arrive? When did the pain start?
Do you know how this machine works? Which one?

*

Associates cookies with sculpture
Cookies are small sculptures
Cookies are not just flat pictures
You have to look at their sizes, their tops,
their sides, their bottoms, their backs
If the cookies are well sculpted they should come
alive for you

My eyes don't sleep well, they stay open

*

Handwriting a thing from the past is all thumbs now

Looks away from screens for a moment and thinks
aloud

This is you inside

Metals conjoined in blue flame

We devoured ourselves

A tower

A snowy distraction

Vibrating between two states beginning to make
an audible hum in the reality of our day. The news is
breaking, is breaking us apart

We are hardwired to forget, to live alongside the
beast as it oppresses

It is power that repeats not history

*

Meaning:

A E I O U know what I mean

I might not ever handwrite again

A tunnel of letters wait to be called on

Slowly it forms or how sweet the sound

Now with one hand, the monster offers pamphlets
to eat and with the other snatches our young

Ain't doing nothing to brag about.
He was a Disciple, a brick out of the pyramid

*

I was too busy looking for a pen

I need an invention band. Color is tough, I know
Money is poison

The buoyant

The delta is open for a moment,

which means its interior ministry is leaking out

Rest your eyes, I forget. Help! Not really
Distinctions between the Lindy and Jitterbug

Skywriting is here then it's gone

Like how babies are little clocks

Anxious, she was anxious. Yeah, yeah, ok. She was
over here. She come up, she come up. She wanted
to know where she wanted to go. She was young
and she was anxious - she was into that. She found
you. She was out there. Really

Sobbing over the spilling milk

The book is ready and includes reviews of
astronauts

A pig with a nice suit. He's an interesting pig

An edgehog
My son had an edgehog but we had to get rid of it

*

LET ERROR
LET TERROR
LETTER ERROR
LETTER TERROR
LETTERROR:

AXQX
BYRY
CZSZ
DATA
EBUB
FCVC
GDWD
HEXE

From seeing to seething
From reading to writhing

*

Mr. Chimenez

She says, I love those gizmos on your face, referring
to his smile

What do you want to hear?
Just put on some human lunch music

My father owned a tobacco factory

He received rain into his body

Feeding malice into the mind

We're like that - a family made from sky

Says I'm an old man now, I can even read lips

My head feels like rock wrapped in rags sinking into
water

Says you need spunk, good radiation, in the morning

What's in their heads there across the street?

Ladders that lead somewhere and chatter, lots of
chatter

Staring at marks on paper

It is so dangerous that even the surface can drown
you

To participate is to make deconstruction more
difficult

That said

Ask Karol to talk about the differences between
Elvis and Picasso
Caravaggio and Mozart
Warhol and Dylan

Distance
is here
The way it
moves in

Says it's an audio flip-book of echoes

Those
corners of fog will
only on occasion
prick your finger

It leads
to a face
of lethargy
and empty stares

It is a breath rehearsal

It's the idea of carrying books around. I've carried
them for decades. Also, memory and nostalgia is
changing, and too, how we store information.

Though, of course, the pleasure of a physical
book is wonderful...

He was anti-library, against all shelving, and hostile
toward anything related to spines

What am I fighting against? Hello?
Two absolute zeros.
One non-solid zero and one non non-solid zero

It was the fault of my name.
Father says I'm ill, god says I'm sick

I've got circles in my head.
I'm sorry, there must've been some green in that
shirt I couldn't register.
I should've trusted you
Eat your food, there are children starving
in West Virginia

Dry bones in a casket.
Removing the pen while stealing it

Speaking with two different tones of lipstick

Ach ya…, the pains of having been, not an
illustrator, but a what!? A German Wood! Umbilical
pause! Treachery? Looking really good moving
through eternity

Frederico Chimenez is the owner of a tobacco
factory

*

KAROL:

The Fitness Spa 2 Chapter 1
Trying to educate beginners to be old
but the reality is
a rough beyond reality
that looks easy
needs a skiff of a well-built gong

What's it like being the youngest
and a person in a 4, a fitness cast.
The only over 40, over minus 5,
youngest in a fitness class – the only complete
"spaz" The only over 50 – a class of elder abs class
– remarks like... This is making my fitness person
proud. He thinks, perhaps, that he will like me
better on my abs. He is not going to do that and
will remain the kindly over 50 in the class.
Thereby one whose abs get high scores where
the least talented and spa-stick doesn't get a big
hand for being a "spaz" Someone now can't
remember if spa-sticks are trying and awesome,
the spa-stick venoms. I can't remember what a
good competitor is, what a hopeless loser is and
she doesn't really give a shit

Roast Beef with mild potholes
garlic for flavoring
this is boring for more colors
then take it out of the box

2 hours at 350 minutes
6lb roast – 6 potatoes
Roast until done
until it's fucking done
Eat
Wash dishes

My first broken leg: I was walking down 1st Avenue
– limping actually - because a truly stupid person
thought that was a hilarious prompt

So I was limping up the street, the walking getting
more difficult every few minutes While waiting for
a light to change, I stuck out my leg rehearsing the
way I would walk across the street - putting as little
pressure on my leg as possible I think this is
getting funnier only if Jerry had the assignment
then my facial expressions would be telling the
whole story

Neutral
fire-minded
or the fence
even-minded

Job needed – all requirements
Job experience – specialities
good at everything
lungs welcome
good with kids
good with elderly (especially small children)
good with all ask people
Specialist!
All locations
all hours
Good diagnosticians!

*

I'm tired, but interested
What does that apply to?
Talking more and more about less and less

The brain is in jeopardy
You can't deny it

When a flugelhorn is a map
They borrow their moods from each other

One point of Privilege seems to be the ability to
look down at others w/o any accountability and
being immersed in the foggy untruth of
convenience, Don't forget convenience

An and too
An A and an other
this that and the other
The bastard of the Chaucer of the ember
Who's that small judge in the mirror?

Yes, I used a child's computer microscope
And yes, materials were prepared beforehand
and yes each video was created under the
influence of different drugs

This lack of enthusiasm can't be condoned
or cordoned off
so perhaps it's chemical

My appointment fell on the floor.
Can you please get me another

The ballot box vs the box office

Purity is in jeopardy too

Higher heights
Higher heights

A coin-operated encounter

Gestures erode
Subtlety dismantles
It's become more brutal than that

The letters are going to kill you and soon

It's not an uncertain sound
This weirdness applied to routine
A champion of paragraphs
riddled with openings

"No foul play here, whatsoever"

*

A hybrid consciousness
That sidesteps gnashing rocks
The removal of radical playground hierarchy

There's a simplicity
I want your spine to rotate

I'm about to clock out, but I should've clocked out
three years ago

Ham
Hey turkey
Swiss cheese
Yes butter
Bacon
Cereal
Two cans Diet Coke
When can ginger ale
It ails for thee

We're upon a threshold that will force us to
reinvent the very nature of how we see and spend
time

The delivery system was strategic deception itself

This awareness is freshness-dated and will start to
stink real soon

The concept of a page though, that's an old one
Looks something like this

*

A man, a mister, a red

The light's on and the dark is on

Burn the blues, yes sir

That's your Saturday face on Monday.
Mr Sun, I beg you, come out

Oh crunch. It's very good for money. You're sleepy.
No, I will not remove my foot. I have one too, one
too

I use this hand cause I'm crooked
if it's not the east then it's the west

What's your favorite animal?
Western Union, no
New Jersey, no
German Shepherd, yes

Look at that box. I'm going to make it
move with my mind

Well, I know her mother was the devil

The judge said to me, if you feed them long
enough they start looking like you

*

That holy man set fire to his mattress last night

Logical fingers
Unique probability
The seven unique probabilities

The thread of inclinations

To continue without interruption, without a direct
threat to you

It is tantamount to lying and you know how I feel
about that

*

Listen to yourself
Listen to yourself..

The world is big
The world is big

I like rain
I like rain...

I like running through the fields
I like running through the fields...

I want to see the volcano at night
I want to see the volcano at night...

I see stars
I see stars...

*

I want to release my exhausted clutch on information

Just in case I bump into a voter who needs
assuaging, arm-twisting or rigorous brain stabbing
 to switch their vote

Don't frighten him, let him keep patting your
shoulder and let him keep talking

Rubber cookies and the truck drivers

Are all being dumped on the Internet
at an alarming rate

It's on the verge of annihilating itself
for the next big thing - whatever that'll be

I want to eliminate and then replace words

Happy with whatever damage we have managed
to inflict upon the word

Thankful to pong

I really wanna know what it's like to stick a feather
into the top half of your new crazy snow

Those threads intersect
Create points in space
Help navigate even the most mundane task

*

So to repeat.
Hey writing, I don't know you anymore

*

I had a horse and it's name was SkyBlue

We opened the first moon

COSMO
It's the name of the first great-grandson

I thought of him first, his safety - to travel safely
below the trophies. That's what's needed. There
are no words for this

You say this in order to capture all the sweets

Captain, we're going for a dry swim and we have
some anxieties about the future. Our homes
should be clean. You should be good and clean
and just

Someone heard her arm. Someone raised their
arm

Now, open your body

Your light
And your poison
Intermingle

You will find the road
That leads to the road
And we'll meet there

Don't tell the police
Please don't tell the police
It's our secret

Find that beautiful place
And stay there
Bring your children there

I will look for you
And I will see you
Everyday

Goodbye my bright one
Goodbye to the family
Goodbye everyone

Voir Dire

UNFINISHD

This
is getting to me

A pile-up of information

You pay for a certain
type of experience

It's subcutaneous
It's here

To choose not to decide is
the least satisfying
and yet we let it happen
over and over again

You resist sacrifice
even if it's for the greater good

Trouble is only reversible
never a tripled thing

What's not attributable
is your fault

Something is not going right

You think I'm talking about it

Weaker than thou
is the voting booth

Yet another required update

It's the small beauties
your eyes catch

Be mindful and
apologize when you're not

Otherwise, go about your business

You can delete me

I don't mind how
other fingers follow the way you dance

It's dancing, what do you want?

But some of me
will stay in your cheek bones

Even after I'm done

A little bump in my step then

You can delete me
It's alright

I built that palace
for you
Whenever you need
And it's full of love and time and snot and smells

It's been a quagmire since
A crushed compass and the discard of words

It happened
It happened twice
It happened three times

I'm some kind of lucky
A dead person
A star of the neighborhood
That's for sure
A whimsy on an otherwise
static surface

I'm being looked at
I'm being noticed
The very letters of the word standout
So that a gaggle of letters matter better than a
word and a word is nothing but a sign of things

You know what I'm saying
You hear intention
Even without a body attached

It's subcutaneous
It's here

A handwritten ghost of moments

It's too much at times
You know it

DRAPES

We are heading
Toward
Global uniformity
In a universal leotard

A Prolonged Stare

Letters careen
Spirals are forming
What's verbal is being
Erased by what's visible

Trumble thru the tranglion bramble to reach
a clearing house of it

To say what happens is an exercise in observation.
To see the happening is a form of talking. I will do
both

In the book
It's the eyes
That meet the words
First
Yes, it's an object
You fuckhead
Both noun and verb

Shovel the glimpse

You're the interesting one
No, you are

The nose

Is Thanatos
Is a scuffle between the prone and the upright letters
of an entrance
Any entrance

I stared, I took my glasses off, I cleaned the lenses,
I rubbed my eyes, but the stars in the sky kept jiggling

The devil they surmised is in the details of the letters
inside the word that stands for an object till that word
becomes the object in your mind

What do you see?

Shapes, patterns, sequences, varying sizes, varying
textures, symmetry, asymmetry, depth, environmental
consequence, regularity, irregularity, color, shading,
cognitive potential, arousal, reflection, contrast,
intention, message, juxtaposed entities, mindless
filigree, poignant decoration, the organics, the quiet
inorganic, tried and true design, hapless shelters,
clues, function, injustice, elegance, resistance,
deformity, brainwashing, acceptance, imbalance,
severe angles, soft corners, miniatures, the
amorphous, the miasmic, beauty, pictures in the
mind, your face my dear one, my dear ones,
altogether and in singularity

A holy unreal electric discharge

Blue and coin and tune and pine. Sentence

mutation, a stacking of h and one elaborate Q
Those e's through the navel. Pearl rain, ape
handprint and compression always collecting
dust. I will tear your eyes out. Language trapped
behind the drape, language in space - the pre
word

Nothing to shake
The focus
Honed in like
A peripheral
Detached from the assembly

Typographic poems and how sound affects font

It's
Poems have
Really exhausted
Their usefulness

It's not
It comes to
No typed words
Reach paper

Anachronism
Spread across
A blank page

Paper is now noise
Language spewing out the mouth
The flecks of which we fashion into new alphabet
And that is never enough to document a real
sensation

It falls

It falls away
It falls
And the image is caught in reflection
The mirror
The wheels
A gray-draped fabric
Nothing stops vibrating

Perhaps we practice for the disintegration

I don't mind

In this scenario
Headlights through dark
The sound of heavy breath
From the dog the cellphone
From the house itself

It's not easy to muster
The kind of silence
The busywork of chemical reaction
In fact, it's impossible
Well, nearly so

I miss my son and my son, so much room to
spread out with not a whisker of trouble to pluck
or plugged crown to impede

If I had daughters, how altered would my lack of a
sister echo through this house

I love my boys, my nut jobs, they affect my love
different and different.

I have learned and leaned on them and they know
little of shifts I've seen

RETINAL BOSS

The language of the stars
and a brief moment of transition captured

The speechevent occurs
In an instant

To return to the molecules of language
To sift through what may still remain
To rummage through the remnants and vestiges

The situation is not in the text
but before and outside and
after and away
The text can only refer to itself - It is not the actual
text but a recollection or
abbreviation of the event
It is not present
but a projection

The alphabet itself is
a metaphor

To be free to fly through a universe of letters
To destroy the sensible and
stable order that contains
this supreme endeavor
To submerge a holy text
until it no longer leaves
any guarantee of meaning

The hum of bees
The hum of a tune
The hum of a plane
The hum of the fridge

A simultaneous overlap
The merge of nature, machine and flesh
The massage or squeeze or manipulation of language
Of any recognizable material
To reach satori
by calculated stimulation
When words fail you
and pictures of the future emerge
When syllables disappear
and communal networks bring
the noise of everyday anonymity

They were accepting proposals on what letters
could be used for besides printing words

An absence of language
A future event

To gather the sensory organs
To disappear depressions
To liberate the body with
electric euphoria

Contrived code vs natural image
Artificial symbol vs organic material

Your basic cartoon morality

This is more than permutation
This is past that

Wring out the smallest elements
Wring out the letters and see what's left

Now go past that

Past the new poem being a visual object
Past the silent reading of typography
Past the ideogram
Past imagetext

The text makes us think
the poet is seeing words
That the eye is doorway
and unlocks the text
in a grand transduction event

As phanopoeia
Where words conjure to convey
an image of an object

Becoming other in distress
and exploration

A tank filled with fire
Ready to engage new terrain

To go past
the lexical world

THE WAITING ROOM

There is no pleasure if if. Capital A and capitol Ism. The moment a reader dislocates their eyes to see language, its material, happening. An untwisted poetics that both captures and documents the letter in its pre and post word condition. It's a snake that reconvenes or a strategy to not get entirely subsumed by the image. The visual machinations transgress or reads seeing or writes vispo or some such hubristic yammer. I've got scarring

To conjugate a gaze
The pronouns of stare
Nosotros are seeing this
The environment is something you bump into

To step up to the box
To make your way into and through the box
Essentially, to disappear
To emerge in a new location
in an unexpected
environment

This position
Is never of my choosing
I am constantly responding
To what comes my way

A position
Will diminish after
Time

One position
Depends on
The many before it
To survive

The position
Was so radical as to
Unravel the entire fabric
Of what came before

His position
Emanated from a center
No one could
Conceive of

These positions
Seem to constitute
An organized front

Her position
Distracted
The others

Their positions
Were designed
To keep them
In power

Two positions
Remained an obstacle
To reaching
A satisfactory
Result

The position
We gathered around
Had an insurmountable
Flaw

Their position
Was not negotiable

The uncanny nature of the eye to misjudge then
right itself. That instant an eye cannot locate
information. A revisiting of early development
and the brain in a frenzy to categorize its external
environment. The eye becomes complacent and
sensory transduction freaks out when the
unprecedented comes in contact with our body
That one wonky second when the brain doesn't
know how to process incoming information. It's
that that I love, it's what drew me from writing to
seeing writing to reading seeing. I seek that
occurrence

Got Stuck/Get Stuck I get in conflict - the
dilemma of using words to convey the reality of
letters - waiting for a future language event - being
here, stuck using words

Children develop in a particular way. They draw
letters then they comply to writing letters. Hand
drawing vs handwriting alphabet. The keyboard is
now eliminating this difference

Uuuuuu double Uuuu
"lifts the veil from the hidden beauty of the world and
makes familiar things as if they were not familiar"
Percy Shelley

Hello? What's your name? My name is Nico
 Vassilakis. Can you spell that out for me, please?
Sure, it's N-I C-O V as in Victor A-S-S-I-L-A-K-I-S.
The sounds still hidden and tucked inside the word

The letters like an off-grid dinosaur lumbering and
uttering, keeping our early developmental selves
alongside our adult frame

I understand, it would be worse than dial-up to
hold a conversation by spelling out each word, by
mouthing each letter

Go ahead, try it with a friend for even a minute and
you'll be like, this is stupid.

I D-O N-O-T W-A-N-T T-O D-O T-H-I-S A-N-Y-M-O-R-E.

And you'd be right

Forgetting is one way to move forward

The changing of the verb

The child was using her finger, as a pencil, trying
to draw letters on an iPad. The O was an
amorphous lake.

Her h was a kind of sad leaning skyscraper.
Not too long after that subway ride, the top part of
her O will meet and touch the solid line, while the
h will bend correctly at the perforated line. There
will be a kind of new perfection achieved

The child will have gone from drawing letters, a
playful expression, to conform to writing

Drawing is a primitive expression of marking
space with time. Writing, or alphabet, is a forced
societal construct

Cursive, in English, is no longer taught, so any
drawing element or personality you find in
handwriting is found in a person's signature

It intends to distract the reader long enough to remind her, she is SEEING text. Poets want to undermine existing social texts, the texts that surround them, by creating and reveling in the new SUBJECTIVE ILLEGIBLE. I couldn't find the language at first, but worked my way through the bullet points slowly. We fit, you and I, perfectly. A string of little bells and a clutch of index cards. I like the alphabet, as a concept and as an A. Genres have blended, groups have formed other groups, etc. That is fabulous news, of course, but what does it mean? Convulsed hands trying to convey some idea - from thought through hand to written form - an electric discharge expressed. I find it interesting, in a way I don't fully comprehend. We no longer live in a place. The experience of living occurs a few feet off the ground. Translating common sound into common sight can be treacherous. Translating common anything into common everything can be treacherous. The child loses her untethered innocent approach for a more rigid, grid-like imitation. For the sake of uniformity, writing alphabet is forced on the child. The viewer can't know what happens. I had to rethink what clapping hands is. Dear Poetry, the thing about you seeming important is that you think you're everywhere. The pleats are naturally hammered back into place. The rock is shaped by water. A sentence, a weft, passes over and below its warp. Hands running under blankets. A magnification of

parts of letters, the parts that no longer resemble
and cannot be traced back to the original and so
have determined to make a go of it on their own.
It will be interesting to see where all the threads
arrive. Ready for that something new, pressured by
what's new. An image lingers. Move these
parentheses around. Remove this parenthesis.
What motifs are common, which types are familiar,
recognizable and repeated. The star-break should
come down a space

To take a snapshot To disrupt To capture the letters just before To isolate pre word activity

The conflict between drawing and writing letters is made more extreme with the presence of a keyboard. There is less opportunity to draw letters as a developmental step for the child. Children will simply tap letters out without engaging alphabet

The space between drawing and writing letters where the verb changes, is the segue that attracts me. The child is free, then the child is locked, then the child is free again

A child should create their own alphabet from their initial forays into drawing - the assigning a glyph to an object

There is no correction correct way to apply reapplication logic to situations imbued with a history historical repetition of cultural social domination except to say correct way to follow the human condition and its to seek power the kind that suffocates subordinates as viewed by empowered enclaves of wealth gatherers so much so that great great great grandchildren are without financial stressors solely on the ability to secure money via policing pro militia bankers paid to fortress the fortress with the particular affected isolation that promotes more desire and more elite thinking toward the other the other person the other person doing those things that allow one to charge five ten twenty fifty times more than cost and cost is advertised as a show of power if applicable to your class your classroom of like minded egos of your desire to rise to be seen to have admiration steered to the way of climbing ladders climbing power to where the loss of connection becomes justified because look how hard you have worked and what you have gathered around you through that effort and see the lower the lesser as disabled in some way and so too continued power dynamics are ever caught in looking up looking down looking out for how the viewer views the viewed and on so and on so

LETTERS ARRANGE THEMSELVES –

It's never a word first

SEEING :
WRITING

LETTERS

"My work constitutes an attempt to immortalize fleeting moments... I must seize the very instant in which the living experience seeps on to the symbol, which in this case is the letter." *Mira Schendel*

*

What are you looking at when you're looking at what you're looking at. The only material is Seen. Only the material is Seen. Seen, unseen, what an eye might see. Two e's, two e's, s_ _n to be. The eye will track. The orb will float till it finds its oar and focused boat. Seeing the former left behind, a past tense of alphabets touching aqueous humor. A sequence comprised entirely of having seen and seeing it too

*

These alphabet parts seek a vision to upend
everything that came before

*

How to proceed...these explorations and explanations are ancillary and redundant to a singular encounter with visual poetry. A definition that undulates in water fluctuates in its own meaning. These accounts attest to failure that never concludes

There's a word for just about everything, but there ain't a word for this

How letters release from their word and what they find themselves doing before and after forming into words. Letters are free to arrange themselves any way they want. For a moment they're autonomous and independent with no restrictions, so they navigate or are drawn toward one another in order to form new and unrealized results

*

Letters seek liberty from word supremacy. Will detach from word and roam the page. Will find new designs to thwart their word captor. Will unhinge entirely and emerge alongside natural formations. Only then. Will the letters offer to return, to reconvene. Will reassemble. Will reenter the word template. Will be poured into WORD meaning, the slots of which letters attend

*

My fascination with how letters sit beside each
other and patiently wait to be freed of their word
logic scrum hasn't subsided. So, I capture that
alphabetic dalliance as document of some future
language event. Vispo is a byproduct of ones
experience with literature, with writing, reading
and seeing. It's about how you look and read your
way passed words and re familiarize yourself with
the intentional drawing of letters

The first tendency of Letters, when newly released
from their word bondage, is to become decorative.
This is usually followed by design logic and visual
pun, as well as other compositional templates.
Next, Letters either proceed into new visual
poetics or return to the word. We are taught to
return, but are seldom given an option. Yes, they
said, let us go, free us

*

Vispo is writing that exploded and reconvened into another form of seeing. Reading this result is openness, writing this new seeing is one way to transmogrify language.

I see no reason to destroy word, I simply want to undo word so the letters become revealed. Letters gather in a pre word formation, free to move about and explore before they are forced to line up and take their place in a word sequence I see the letters as ingredients without which words would not exist. Words are a form of convenience. They take the place of an object in language. Letters are the math that allows this equation to result in words. We wipe our memory clean of letters and allow words to fill the air. The information letters house has become lost to us

A visual poem is successful when it makes alternative use of writing and devalues the sequence of alphabet typically reserved for word communication, and offers a visual logic to how letters can be presented. I am particularly interested in letters, but more so, I am involved in the pieces of letters that just barely hang on to recognizable form before being jettisoned into new terrain. This terrain is part of the development of language or pre/post language.
How children are first asked to draw and then to write letters. It moves from free expression in drawing to rigid grid-like writing that makes everything the same. Children are forced to comply to group communication before they are ever encouraged to create their own alphabet.

*

My work could look like a document or field-recording of my unconscious, but more than anything it is a capture shot of letters before or after they formulate into word. Letters have a life unto themselves

> *"...letters have a destination other than words."*
> *Isidore Isou*

My overall concept about this is that we are on the planet to find a way to leave the planet. We are exhausting the planet's resources and so technology or the language of technology must take its necessary path, must reach a conclusion. Human beings, in their current condition, will consume the very means that sustains them. We will have no choice but to explore off-planet solutions.

Technology is a problem we live with, a problem we absorb and adjust to as we go along. Nature is the great equalizer. Nature is an alphabet we have forgotten, because convenience has made us soft and helpless. Also, the idea of generating constant profit has degraded our integrity. Being a poet, a real poet, has become near impossible in this world. Too many other concerns have made us into hybrid poets, living as poets in tangential situations. How are we able to maintain focus in this accelerated environment?

*

Hello letters! - you will leave your words, will be unattached, able to drift into all new visible features of experience.

A sequence of energy constants:

a) The discharge of a word is finally equal to the energy found in its letters

b) Now make those same letters askew, reposition them on a page, have the letters touch other letters in unaccustomed ways--the energy is the same

c) Then cut the letters in half and use their visual elements as the available material to construct or compose the new vispo

THE NEW SACCADE

It seems like this very night I am losing the alphabet

Are we expected to succumb to these fascist markings?

Where is this non arbiter-based template? What is the new visual meter?

"and to me letters are virtual particles, giving up their golden treasures of significant/insignificant travels."
bill diMichele

There are sequences that create visual conflict, capture opposing forces, riff on phrases and structures and signal possible manifestos. One tries to navigate notions, locations, materials and explore a framework for how visual poetry or writing can be a readable experience with some consequence.

To humbly thank you again for your eyes and how they work.

Pieces of letters or visual graphemes carry thot. What are the parameters of reading seeing? Does the work inform the reader/viewer on how much to see, how much to look for? We're at the viewers mercy, I suppose, as to what excites them enough to engage further. You can't know what you can't know. Submerged into the word I am tracing the outline of its letters. A sequence comprised entirely of having seen and seeing it too.

The aleatory and rigid markings, the dance of the
letter captured, the as-of-yet unrealized alphabet

The "dirty" vispoems continue, the fortunate
mishaps, the haphazardly arranged, finding the
parts or points that attract deviation.

*

In this situation
your eyes are all lowercase

A single letter on the wall. A couple words while
 walking. Three phrases on an escalator.

This position in line is fucking untenable

An ice cube sliding off my palm. Diagramming the
sentence, finding a way to get where you'd like to
be. Yes, these narratives will collide, but not before
tearing us apart -- two separate flags demanding
allegiance. Where the primitive one is the
successor and not merely the first.

*

A tunnel of letters wait to be called on

The captured space inside a letter

Take, for instance, the uppercase B

An enclosure, a bubble or bubbles where history
is held

Your nose above water

An iteration of roundness in nature

Among the linear sharps
A celestial interface awaits

*

Time keeps folding into smaller and shorter
intervals

Holding onto one dimension
too tight
To wheel free of an issue
And drawn to
the other
I will become you
Hesitate
Hesitate
Let's go
Will wear
your template
till it fits no longer
Will pour out buttonholes

Twigs touch
Limbs bend
A fractal maze
no weather can quell
Disaster will not harm me
until it annihilates me

Like electrons, letters exhaust combinatory
possibilities to achieve newer and better results

The issue with L is H

The word is a visual translation

Desperate to splice slivers of letters
into the fresh and unforeseen

*

Handwriting an irritation

If you strike at beauty, aim at something else

A transformed writing is technology itself

The language of itself without irony

NOTES ON LETTERS

Good morning everyone, we're all here today
attending our local *Letters of Leisure Society*
meeting

The first point of order; to stop our eyes, "my eyes
want out"

I pick a flyer up off the ground
Something about a SYMPOSIUM ON VISUAL
POETRY in two weeks

"The constellation of letters is similar to other
constellations, words in a sonnet, natural
formations included."

*

Wait, I am trying to anchor myself
Maybe I cannot, maybe I do not want to

Teasing the Alphabet - Words to Come! zaum zin
zoooooo mow moon!!!!

All language, everywhere, from all times, all
seasons, coming to a glorious messy end in the
biggest, blackest full stop ever

It's like a neurological trick
Letters and flowers
The collapse of words?

Definitely something! Perhaps a very strange and
particular tree in a special setting
I think it is kicking in....

Seems these letters, primarily the g & f, are having
a flamboyant interlude before gravity draws them
down into word formation

Dude, your letters are like a charcuterie

Singing letters noising their wail into the weird
wor(l)d

My new favorite!
8 windows. I see you

A variety of single letters were used to compose
this piece, as well as words like literature, sleep,

letters, and phrases such as pharmaceutical
language adjustment and trapped by decorative
tendencies. Also a few punctuation marks.

Uh oh. What's that in the middle?
The curtain, the background of letters and
florescent fish with a touch of pink Venetian blinds

Pearls fall from a typewriter.
Lovely jellyfish language moving upward through
the See

Are they scattering and lifting away, or circling in,
unstoppably?

Upper limit ligature.
Tottering insect vispo.
A "word wing spreader."

And now this one is my favorite!

When there's nothing else to do, go gold. Rococo!
Letter pores in the epidermis of words.
The type is so tight, I can't breathe.
"Periodic table of speech" Voila!

*

The letters defy word. They detach and leave word
unstable. The letters, tired of adjusting to word, are
free to roam and construe

Yes, it's certainly a catch. Words are dented, letters
lack cohesion, intentional markings are flaccid, yet
we swim on. We explore our fascinations. I bring
it up as a dilemma I cannot resolve and am happy
not to, but find my thoughts returning to again and
again

Otherness. The waste of time is enormous, but I'm
guessing is become an aspect of my identity and
not so easy to discharge

> *"You should leave here wanting all letters
> liberated of their word scrum obligation"*

My choices, my decisions fluctuate, but they always
intend to convey a letter in flight, spinning free
before ultimately settling into a static word

They function as an alternate method of seeing
and result in unexpected ways of reading These
letters are then freed to interact in unprecedented
ways. Otherwise, I am left floating in a room
waiting for something to catch my eye

To restate it; the act of staring at a word will
release the letters that comprise it. Some of them
are on my side, some of them think I'm guilty

Letter fragments, even those aleatory markings,
come together to assume this new meaning.

What these images say and where they are
going...

*

Mostly from a fidget, a doodle, a juxtaposing of
material and being visually dyslexic

It's pieces of letters that carry thought

*

A cobbler of alphabet

I use my finger gliding across the screen
to articulate and sustain an idea.
A contoured cursive writ in letters

*

Dissimilar time signatures. Things that make sense as needed. It tends to unfold the way a viewer thinks about seeing. Walking next to oneself. Words curtailed, pictures condensed, reaching a visual capture of happenstance and the associative properties found therein. Amputation here is a forced shortening, snippets alongside details. *"Things which coincide with one another equal one another."*

SI SI SI SI SI SI SI
SI   SI
SI   SI
SI   LENCE   SI
SI   SI
SI   SI
SI SI SI SI SI SI SI

The text designs a landscape you are invited to
engage in. The vocabulary provides the audience
a setting to move through

*

The circle is everything, is everywhere. A word is made, collapses, then reforms endlessly. Letters glisten and play over the surface of our eye. They make the word one letter at a time while forming word signage for our convenience. They are in a whirl caught before ever organizing into a word. Bits of letters on excursion, rows of punctuation in frolic with the guiding premise that words disintegrate. Most people consider words devalued by visual deterioration as the destruction of language. I see the release and rise of the Letter Empire. Each letter a sound, a thought, a visual concept that houses our human history. Letters are always on the verge of combining into words. But what if they were never to reach that result? I went no ow say this you.

Gja frun koltk 'deyp wwqh olf. H s R gh x -u tt L. Vvv e w(o OQa z

 Nico Vassilakis is a poet who writes and draws language that focuses on the visual jettisoning of letters from their word position. He has published books of poetry and text/art including *Disparate Magnets* (BlazeVOX), *Alphabet Noir* (c_L Books), *Moments Notice* (Luna Bisonte), *Diesel Hand* (Chax Press), *Text Loses Time* (ManyPenny) *and Diptychs (Otolith). He co-edited The Last Vispo Anthology: Visual Poetry 1998-2008 (Fantagraphics) and was a curator of several international visual/concrete poetry exhibitions. He currently lives in Greenville, IL with his wife and animals.*

SIE
DU